Natural Health Guide

Herbs, Herb Formulas and other Natural Remedies

Revised Second Edition

By Deanne Tenney

Natural Health Guide

© 1994 by Woodland Health Books

Published by
Woodland Health Books
P.O. Box 160
Pleasant Grove, Utah 84062

Printed in the United States of America
ISBN 0-913923-81-8

Notice to the Reader:

The information contained in this book is for educational purposes only. It is not intended to be used to diagnose any ailment or prescribe any remedy. It is not meant to be a substitute for professional help. It is intended to set forth historical uses of natural remedies. A person should consult a duly approved health professional for any condition which requires their services. This information is not intended as a substitute for qualified medical care.

Neither the author nor the publisher directly or indirectly dispenses medical advice or prescribes the use of natural remedies as a form of treatment. The author and publisher disclaim any liability if the reader uses or prescribes any remedies, natural or otherwise, for him/herself or for another.

Table of Contents

Table of Remedies

Introduction

Today more and more people are becoming inter-ested in the field of Natural Health. As controversy over prescription and over-the-counter drugs contin-ues, individuals are seeking alternative methods of healing. The use of natural remedies is increasing in popularity as people rediscover their natural health heritage.

In fact, many medical doctors recognize the bene-fits of natural methods of treatment including herbs, vitamins, minerals, natural remedies, and nutrition. Scientific studies are being conducted involving nutritional approaches to healing. These studies con-firm the healing powers of natural methods.

Herbalists see nature as a positive force in healing the body. Herbs, vitamins, minerals, and natural remedies provide the body with nutrients to help the body avoid disease and aid in the body's efforts to heal itself.

Maintaining good health should be everyone's goal. The natural approach to healthy living helps the body fight and prevent illness. Herbs can help bal-ance the body's chemistry helping to avoid disease. Herbs and natural remedies can provide energy and encourage proper blood circulation to eliminate toxic accumulations and congestion that cause disease. The natural approach to health can help the body heal itself limiting the side effects common to treatment based solely upon synthetic drugs.

This **Natural Health Guide** describes certain herbal and other natural remedies traditionally used to foster good health and combat unhealthful conditions in the body.

Leading Natural Formulas

1.   BALANCED HERBAL WEIGHT CONTROL
      FORMULA

INGREDIENTS: Ma Huang; Salix Alba and Fucus
                Vesiculosis.

USES: This weight control; formula is all-natural and spe-
cially-formulated to provide a well-balanced, healthy
approach to weight control. Each of the ingredients is care-
fully selected and combined to work together to become a
powerful tool to help increase energy and maintain proper
weight. Balance is a key factor in achieving optimum
weight. This formula can help the body maintain a proper
balance allowing it to function well. This formula can help
the body reduce the size of the fat cells through thermogen-
esis. This process helps increase energy while stored
reserves of fat are burned causing weight loss, if necessary.
It aids the body to encourage the burning of fat. It is well
established that the overweight body is not as healthy as it
could be. Extra weight creates strain on the cardiovascular
system and the other systems of the body. Weight reduction
can be achieved by putting into proper balance body systems. Many people have found that the proper combination

of these ingredients helps achieve an effective weight-loss program resulting in an improved body weight and, therefore, a healthier body.

2.   HERBAL WEIGHT CONTROL PLUS

INGREDIENTS: Glycine L-Methionine in a base of herbs.

USES: This formula is helpful with the weight loss process. This combination is thought to suppress the appetite, to help with weight control. It is helpful in preventing excess accumulation of fat in the liver. It also aids in the control of fat levels in the blood and in the prevention of cholesterol buildup.

3.   WEIGHT LOSS TEA

INGREDIENTS: Senna, Buckthorn, Peppermint, Caa Inhem, Uva Ursi, Orange Peel, Rose Hips, Althea, Honeysuckle and Chamomile.

USES: This combination of natural ingredients is helpful in alleviating constipation. It is a natural laxative. It is also helpful as a natural cleanser and a digestive aid. Many people are concerned with achieving optimum body weight. The proper combination of these herbs is helpful for losing weight as well as aiding the body in maintaining a desirable weight. This unique combination of herbs help the body digest and assimilate nutrients from food. This tea can also help cleanse the body of buildup in the colon which can contribute to digestive problems. It may also help suppress the appetite which helps to eliminate between meal snacking. The tea can also help rid the body of excess water accumulation.

4. ENERGY TONIC/HIGH FIBER DRINK
(lemon or berry)

INGREDIENTS: Fructose, Natural Flavors, Citric Acid, Sodium Bicarbonate, L-Carnitine, Potassium, Calcium, Vitamins, Glucose Polymers, Siberian Ginseng, Gotu Kola, Bee Pollen, and other ingredients.

USES: This powder drink is specially formulated to build muscle tissue, increase energy, and create an over-all feeling of well being. It is useful for athletes in endurance sports and preventing muscle cramping. It is also known to increase energy in the body. It is also helpful with problems such as ADD (Attention Deficit Disorder). It is thought to strengthen the heart and help prevent cholesterol accumulation.

5. WEIGHT CONTROL/ENERGY TONIC

INGREDIENTS: Fructose, Natural Flavors, Citric Acid, Sodium Bicarbonate, L-Carnitine, Potassium, Calcium, Vitamins, Glucose Polymers, Siberian Ginseng, Gotu Kola, Bee Pollen, T64X (special herbs in a lactose base) and other ingredients.

USES: This powder drink, when added to water, helps with weight control. It is also helpful in increasing energy. It is high in fiber which is essential for good health. This formula also contains minerals which help control fluid balance. These minerals also help prevent muscle cramps during exercise. This tonic can aid in sports endurance because of the supply of important vitamins, minerals and glucose polymers.

6. HERB/MINERAL LIQUID

INGREDIENTS: Purified Water, Natural Caramel Color, Glycerin, Potassium Citrate, Calcium Glycerophosphate, Magnesium Glycero-phosphate, Ferric Glycerophosphate, Iodine, Chamomile Flowers, Sarsaparil-la Root, Celery Seed, Alfalfa, Dandelion Root, Horehound Root, Licorice Root, Seneca Root, Passion Palmetto Berry, Angelica Root, Siberian Ginseng, Gotu Kola, Cascara Sagrada, Methylparaben, Potassium Hydroxide, Propylparaben, Natural Mint and Anise Flavors.

USES: The Herb/Mineral Liquid contains vital minerals that give elasticity to muscles, soothe the nerves , normal-ize blood pressure, and strengthen bones and teeth . It also contains herbal extracts that aid in blood purification, bowel conditioning, glandular balancing, and increasing stamina, all of which leads to an overall sense of well-being. It is also considered useful for arthritis, balding, and brain stimulation.

7.   BLUE/GREEN ALGAE

INGREDIENTS: Salt water blue-green algae free from contamination. High in minerals and vitamins.

USES: Blue-green algae is the highest known source of chlorophyll. It is believed to increase the oxygen in the blood which helps build red blood cells. This can help cleanse the liver, bloodstream, and bowels. This combination is high in beta-carotene which is recognized for its nutritional value. This product can help build the immune system which is essential in resisting diseases such as AIDS and cancer. It is also very helpful in increasing energy in the body.

8.   CIRCULATION

INGREDIENTS: Chelated Vitamins, Minerals, Amino Acids, Glandulars, Herbs, Essential Fatty Acids .

USES: This combination is helpful in increasing circulation in the body systems. It can help eliminate toxic metals in the body, lower cholesterol levels, and reduce hypertension. It is helpful in promoting cardiovascular health . This formula is helpful in increasing over-all body health.

9.   CLEANSER PLUS CAPS

INGREDIENTS: Red Clover Blossoms, Sheep Sorrel, Peach Bark, Barberry Root, Echinacea, Licorice Root, Oregon Grape Root, StallingiaRoot, Cascara SagradaRoot, SarsaparillaRoot, Prickly Ash Bark, Burdock Root, Kelp, and Rosemary Leaf.

USES: Many view cancer as a severe disorder of the immune system affecting different parts of the body. These herbs can help cleanse the blood, cleanse deep into tissue and cells, supply energy to the body systems, rid the body of toxic chemicals, help hormone imbalance, increase circulation, and stimulate metabolism. It is thought to help with liver problems, toxins, skin disorders such as acne, eczema, and psoriasis, allergies, Alzheimer's, metabolism and immune related illnesses.

10.   APHRODISIAC/ENERGY (male or female)

INGREDIENTS: Suma, Siberian Ginseng, Damiana, Sarsaparilla, Gotu Kola, Licorice Root, Fo-Ti Herb, Saw Palmetto, Ginger Root, Ho-Shou-Wu, and Nettle.

USES: This herbal formula is valuable in restoring sexual energy. For many centuries different cultures have used natural plant sources to enhance sexual function. This combination of selected herbs can help with hormone balance in the body and, in some cases, even with impotence .

11.   STRESS

INGREDIENTS: Valerian Root, Scullcap, Hops, Thiamine Mononitrate, Riboflavin, Nicotinamide, Calcium Pantothenate, Pyridoxine HCL, Ascorbic Acid, Choline Bitartrate, Inositol, Para-aminobenzoic Acid, Schiz..ndra Chinesis, Piper Methysticum, Folic Acid, Cyanocobalamin, and Biotin.

USES: Stress is a common complaint in our busy lives. This combination contains ingredients helpful for calming the nerves and improving endurance during the pressures of every day live. This natural formula can replenish the body with nutrients lost by stress, illness, work, fatigue, and pressures of life.

12.   NATIVE AMERICAN TEA

INGREDIENTS: Burdock, Turkey Rhubarb, Sorrel, Slippery Elm, and Cress .

USES: This Native American herbal tea is a cleansing formula that is used to benefit the immune system. It is wholesome and aids in strengthening the body. It is thought to help with conditions such as cancer, tumors, diabetes, Lupus, and Epstein Barr .

13.   BLOOD PRESSURE PLUS

INGREDIENTS: Fumitory Knollensonnenblume, Persian
Garlic, Onion, Strawberry Leaves,
Raspberry Leaves, Garlic, Citruce,
Cichorium Intybus, Linn., Pear, Calcome,
Rueprechtskraut , Vite, and Licorice Root.

USES: This combination is thought to strengthen the circulatory system. It can help strengthen the heart and maintain a normal blood pressure.

14.   WATER PURIFIER FILTER

USES: A water purifier filter can cleanse the water we
drink by removing potentially harmful chemicals, bacteria
and heavy metals (such as lead). One system found effective utilizes a three filter system. Clean, pure water is
something we all need and expect. But we cannot depend
on ordinary tap water to be free of all contamination and
harmful elements. A water purifier system can help keep
the water you drink safe.

WEIGHT CONTROL FORMULAS

In a society of plenty, excess consumption and relative inactivity may lead to excessive weight gain. These herbal formulas are designed to help lose weight and help the body regain its natural, healthy balance.

15.   HERBAL WEIGHT CONTROL FORMULA

Ingredients: Ma Huang, Salix Alba, and Fucus Vesiculosis .

USES: An all-natural formula designed to provide a well-balanced, healthy approach to weight control.
See #1, above.

16.   HERBAL WEIGHT CONTROL PLUS
See #2, above

17.   WEIGHT LOSS TEA
See #3 above

18.   WEIGHT CONTROL/ENERGY TONIC
See #5 above

19.   FAT BURNER/LEAN MUSCLE BUILDER/ L-CARNITINE

INGREDIENTS: L-Carnitine, Zinc amino acid chelate.

USES: This combination is designed to build muscle tissue and increase energy. It can help build muscle while reducing fat. It has also helped fight cholesterol build-up and strengthen the heart .

20.   APPETITE SUPPRESSANT (homeopathic)

INGREDIENTS: Anacardium 8X, Ignatia 8X, Graphites 12X,   Antimonium   Crudum   8X, Argnetum Nictricum 8X, Pulsatilla Nigricans 6X, Sepia 8X, Hypothalamus 10X, in 20% alcohol.

USES: This spray contains ingredients which can homeopathically relieve indigestion, help gain optimum body weight, and strengthen the hypothalamus. It is a convenient size to carry along and a quick spray may help suppress the appetite .

21.   METABOLISM

INGREDIENTS: Elemental Manganese, Iodine (kelp), Amino Acids (glutamic acid, proline, histidine).

USES: This unique formula is designed to help increase metabolism which can aid in weight control. These ingredients, properly combined, can help stimulate the body's metabolism allowing it to work more efficiently.

22. OBESITY I

INGREDIENTS: Vitamin B-6, Lecithin, Apple Cider Vinegar, Kelp, Choline, Inositol, Calcium, Magnesium, Juniper Berry, Uva Ursi, and Essential Fatty Acids.

USES: This formula can provide essential vitamins and minerals necessary for proper use of food in the body. As the body uses foods and their nutrients more efficiently, it operates in a healthier manner. It is known to increase energy in the body as well as work as an appetite suppressant.

23. OBESITY II

INGREDIENTS: Parthenium, Chickweed, Licorice Root, Saffron, Gotu Kola, Guar Gum, Cascara Sagrada, Red Clover, Echinacea, Fennel, Black Walnut, Kelp, Dandelion Root, Hawthorn Berries, and Papaya.

USES: This combination is helpful when trying to lose weight. The formula combines ingredients essential to proper nutrition and assimilation of food while stimulating the body.

24.   CHROMIUM

INGREDIENTS: Gymnena Sylvestre, Papaya, and Chromium Picolinate .

USES: This formula is useful for weight control . It also helps with digestion and food assimilation . It is thought to promote body toning. It is used by some for diabetes and related problems of blood sugar and the pancreas .

HERBAL MEDICINES

Certain herbal combinations were assembled with specific health deficiencies in mind. These combinations were aimed at the condition indicated.

25.   ALLERGIES

INGREDIENTS: Concentrated Ephedra, White Willow Bark, Valerian Root, Lobelia, Golden Seal Root, Bee Pollen, and Capsicum.

USES: This allergy combination can help reduce the symptoms associated with allergies and colds such as swollen membranes and congested nasal and sinus passages. It is a natural decongestant that helps the body restore free-breathing.

26. CONSTIPATION/CLEANSING

INGREDIENTS: Cascara Sagrada and Aloe Vera.

USES: This combination works as a natural and gentle overnight laxative. It can help regulate the system and aid the bowels in working properly.

27.   STRESS
See # 11

28.   PMS

INGREDIENTS: Dong Quai, White Willow Bark, Uva
Ursi, Valerian, Juniper Berries, Licorice
Root, DL-phenylalanine, Black Cohosh,
Cramp Bark, and Ginger.

USES: Premenstrual syndrome is a problem for many
women. This formula can help the body relieve the symptoms with natural ingredients. It can help with cramps,
bloating, backaches, irritability and tension common
among PMS sufferers.

29.   ANALGESIC

INGREDIENTS: Extract of White Willow Bark.

USES: White Willow Bark was used anciently to alleviate
pain and discomfort. It is a natural approach to eliminate
the discomfort due to inflammation, tension, headaches,
and fevers .

30. COLD/MUCUS

INGREDIENTS: Extract of Ephedra, Horehound, White
Willow, Licorice Root, Pan Pien Lien,
Chickweed, Mullein, Echinacea, Golden
Seal Root, Cayenne, Wild Cherry Bark,
and Rose Hips.

USES: This formula can help ease the symptoms of the common cold. It can reduce sinus and nasal congestion and reduce the swelling of nasal membranes. It also can help relieve the symptoms associated with a cold. The ingredients can help with the discomfort all cold sufferers feel.

31.   DIGESTIVE AID

INGREDIENTS: Papain, Prolase, Bromelain, Diastase, Amaylase, Anise Seed, Slippery Elm Bark, Golden Seal Root, Fennel Seed, Papaya Leaves and extracts of Chamomile, Peppermint Leaves and Papaya Melon.

USES: This combination can help the body digest and assimilate food. It can help relieve gas, stomach cramps, and bloating which some individuals suffer after eating.

32.   INSOMNIA/NERVOUSNESS

INGREDIENTS: Scullcap Extract, Chamomile Flowers, Valerian Root, Passion Flower Extract, Kava Kava, and Catnip.

USES: Insomnia is a common problem. This formula can help promote relaxation and induce sleep. This natural formula works as a sleep aid to help a person relax and get a good night's sleep helping them function efficiently because of a well rested body and mind.

33.   KIDNEY/URINARY TRACT

INGREDIENTS: Uva Ursi, Juniper Berries, Shavegrass, Cornsilk, Parsley, Queen of the Meadow, Buchu Leaves, Goldenrod, Cubeb Berries, Powdered Whole Cranberries, and Watermelon Seed.

USES: This combination can help relieve the body of excess water which can cause swelling, weight gain, bloating, and puffiness. Excess fluid retention can be very uncomfortable and these ingredients can help eliminate the problem.

34. NAUSEA/ INDIGESTION

INGREDIENTS: Ginger Root, Peppermint Leaves Extract, Anise Seed, and Catnip.

USES: This formula contains nausea fighting ingredients. It can help with nausea and indigestion due to motion sickness, illness or over-eating.

35. ENERGY/STIMULANT

INGREDIENTS: Chinese Herbal Tea Extract, Siberian Ginseng Extract, Gotu Kola Extract, Bee Pollen, Calcium Carbonate, Ascorbic Acid, Potassium, Phosphate, Magnesium Oxide, Kelp, Zinc Gluconate, Manganese Gluconate, D-alpha Tocopherol Succinate, Niacinamide, Copper Gluconate, Ferrous Fumerate, Vitamin A Palmitate, Calcium

Pantothenate, Vitamin D-3, Rose Hips, Pyridoxine HCL , Riboflavin, Thiamine Mononitrate, Folic Acid, Octocosanol, Biotin, and Cyanocobalamin.

USES: This combination can help the body meet its additional nutritional needs caused by extra activity. This formula helps when demands are placed on the body during high activity which may run down the body and may otherwise lead to illness.

36. IMMUNE SYSTEM

INGREDIENTS: Vitamin C (500mg), Odorless Whole Garlic, Zinc Gluconate, Bee Propolis, Echinacea, Concentrated Extracts of Pau d'Arco, Rutin, Golden Seal Root, Selenomenthionine, Peppermint, and Cloves.

USES: This unique formula contains many nutrients vital to the immune system. Our bodies must combat daily the effects of pollution, chemicals, and stress. And this combination can help rid the body of toxins and increase immunity from disease.

HERBAL COMBINATIONS

These combinations of herbs were designed to help the body work properly so as to avoid illness. An ounce of prevention is worth a pound of cure!

37.   ARTHRITIS

INGREDIENTS: Yucca, Willow, Alfalfa, Burdock, Black Cohosh, Sarsaparilla, Parsley, Comfrey Root, Slippery Elm, Redmond Clay, Capsicum, and Pan Pien Lien .

USES: This herbal combination is useful for people suffering from arthritis, bursitis, calcification, gout, and rheumatism. It was designed to reduce inflammation and swelling, relieve tension pain, neutralize uric acid, clean the blood, stimulate circulation and heal sore joints. It can also help aid recovery from joint injuries.

38.   BONE/MUSCLE/CARTILAGE

INGREDIENTS: White Oak Bark, Comfrey Root, Wormwood, Pan Pien Lien, Scullcap, Black Walnut Hulls, Queen of the Meadow, Marshmallow Root, and Mullein.

USES: This herbal formula is helpful in healing bruises, sore joints, and weak connective tissue. It contains herbs rich in minerals which aid in the healing process. It is believed to strengthen the bones, muscles and connective tissue and improve circulation.

39.   BONES/CALCIUM

INGREDIENTS: Oatstraw, Horsetail (Shavegrass), Comfrey Leaves, and Pan Pien Lien.

USES: This formula is high in calcium. It is excellent for strengthening the bones. Calcium is necessary for bone health and this combination also contains herbs containing essential vitamins and minerals which aid in the absorption of calcium. For these reasons, the ingredients in Bones/Calcium may also be useful for balding, fractures, leg cramps and mineral difficiencies.

40.   BLOOD PRESSURE I (high or low)

INGREDIENTS: Capsicum and Garlic.

USES: This herbal formula is useful in enhancing overall circulation, tone and strengthening the heart. It is believed to be useful in stabilizing the blood pressure whether high or low.

41.   BLOOD PRESSURE II (high or low)

INGREDIENTS: Garlic and Parsley.

USES: This herbal formula is helpful to stimulate the circulation of the body and in strengthening the heart.

42.   BLOOD PRESSURE PLUS
   See # 13

43.   COLDS

INGREDIENTS: Bayberry, Ginger, Willow, White Pine, Cloves, and Capsicum.

USES: This formula is beneficial in fighting colds and congestion. It can help aid circulation for rapid healing, helping to fight infections, expel mucus, purify the blood, strengthen the lungs, soothe the stomach, and break-up congestion. It can also help strengthen the immune system to fight disease.

44.   MUCUS

INGREDIENTS: Comfrey Root, Fenugreek, Yerba Santa, Hyssop, and Wild Cherry.

USES: Mucus buildup can cause many problems. This combination of herbs can help rid the body of mucus in the respiratory and lymphatic systems.

45.   BLOOD PURIFIER

INGREDIENTS: Gentian Root, Catnip, Bayberry, Golden Seal Root, Myrrh Gum, Irish Moss, Fenugreek, Chickweed, Comfrey Root, Yellow Dock, Prickly Ash, St. John's Wort, Blue Vervain, Mandrake, Evening Primrose and Cyani Flower.

USES: This herbal combination helps purify the blood, detoxify poisons, increase circulation, eliminate excess fluids and balance the glandular system.

46.   DIABETES/PANCREAS

INGREDIENTS: Cedar Berries, Licorice Root, Uva Ursi, Golden Seal Root, Mullein, and Capsicum.

USES: Cases of diabetes are increasing in the United States. Many attribute this increase to poor nutrition and the resulting lack of essential nutrients. This herbal formula can help heal the pancreas and aid the body in assimilating nutrients essential to the body.

47.   INDIGESTION

INGREDIENTS: Peppermint, Fennel, Ginger, Wild Yam, Catnip, Cramp Bark, Spearmint, and Papaya.

USES: Heartburn, gas and a sluggish feeling can be indications of poor digestion. This formula can help with indigestion by stimulating the digestive process.

48. FEVERS

INGREDIENTS: Fenugreek Seed and Thyme.

USES: Fevers often accompany illness. This herbal combination can help relieve fevers and chills while aiding in healing the body.

49. HAYFEVER

INGREDIENTS: Brigham Tea, Burdock, Golden Seal Root, Parsley, Marshmal-low, Juniper Berries, Capsicum, and Pan Pien Lien.

USES: Millions of Americans suffer from allergic reactions to pollen each Spring and Summer. It manifests itself in watery eyes, itching nose and eyes, runny nose, headaches and sinus aches. Hayfever is like a cold without any relief. The allergic reaction is nature's way of trying to eliminate the toxins. This herbal combination can help clean and strengthen the body and eliminate the annoying symptoms of hayfever.

50. HYPOGLYCEMIA/LOW BLOOD SUGAR

INGREDIENTS: Licorice Root, Juniper Berries, Wild Yam, Dandelion Root, and Horseradish.

USES: Hypoglycemia means low blood sugar. It is associated with drastic mood swings. This herbal formula can supply energy to a weakened system, help the adrenal glands to produce adrenalin and encourages the pancreas to manufacture natural insulin. These herbs also help clean the liver, eliminate acids in the blood and help stimulate and clean the body system.

51.   LAXATIVE/CLEANSER

INGREDIENTS: Buckthorn, Senna Leaves, Psyllium and Fennel.

USES: The Laxative/Cleanser combination is excellent for constipation problems. It aids in cleaning the body of toxic matter that can accumulate in the colon.

52.   LIVER DISORDERS

INGREDIENTS: Dandelion Root, Golden Seal Root, Red Beet Root, Yellow Dock, Bayberry, Oregon Grape Root, and Pan Pien Lien.

USES: The liver manufactures digestive enzymes and acts as a filter between the intestines and the heart. It is important to keep the liver in good working order. This herbal combination can help the liver work properly, provide nutrients for healthy liver function, detoxify poisons, clear liver obstructions and aid in circulation. These herbs are beneficial for the liver and gall bladder.

53.   MENOPAUSE

INGREDIENTS: False Unicorn, Black Cohosh, Blue Cohosh , Cramp Bark , Pennyroyal, Bayberry, Ginger, Squaw Vine, Uva

Ursi, Raspberry Leaves, and Blessed Thistle.

USES: This combination helps provide the necessary nutrients to aid the body in producing natural estrogen. It can also help in controlling hot flashes and mood swings which can accompany menopause. These herbs can help stimulate the adrenal glands, supply energy and aid in depression.

54.   MEMORY PROBLEMS

INGREDIENTS: Lily of the Valley, Periwinkle, Mullein, Juniper Berries, and Pan Pien Lien.

USES: Memory problems can occur at any age but are more prevalent in later years. One of the symptoms of Alzheimer's disease is memory loss. This herbal combination has been reported to increase stimulation to the brain and help clear the mind.

55.   GLANDS

INGREDIENTS: Mullein and Pan Pien Lien.

USES: The combination of Mullein and Pan Pien Lien can help stimulate the glands. It is also useful in cases of asthma, bronchitis, mumps, pleurisy, lymph congestion and tuberculosis.

56.   MINERALS/VITAMINS

INGREDIENTS: Alfalfa, Dandelion and Kelp.

USES: This balance of herbs is high in minerals and vita-mins. It is especially useful when an acidic condition is present in the body.

57.   DIGESTION

INGREDIENTS: Papaya and Peppermint.

USES: Papaya contains papain which is an enzyme that breaks down food protein into a digestible state. Peppermint works on the salivary glands as an aid in digestion. Thus, this combination can aid with digestive problems.

58.   PARASITES

INGREDIENTS: Diatomaceous Earth, Wormwood, and
                Black Walnut.

USES: This herbal combination has been reported to help expel worms and parasites from the body. It can also help provide essential nutrients to the body where they are needed.

59. RESPIRATORY PROBLEMS

INGREDIENTS: Comfrey Root, Mullein, Chickweed, Marshmallow, Slippery Elm, and Pan Pien Lien.

USES: The balance of these herbs can help when respiratory problems occur. They help by healing the lungs and removing mucus, cleaning the blood, soothing the stomach, calming nerves, inducing sleep, reducing inflammation of the mucus membranes and healing cell tissue.

60. APHRODISIAC/ENERGY
See #10

61. HORMONE IMBALANCE

INGREDIENTS: Siberian Ginseng, Sarsaparilla, Black Cohosh, Licorice Root, Periwinkle, Damiana, Alfalfa, and Kelp.

USES: Hormones are chemical regulators of the body's systems. This unique balance of herbs can help when the glandular system is not efficiently producing the hormones needed by the body.

62.   BLOOD PRESSURE

INGREDIENTS: Capsicum, Golden Seal Root, Parsley, Ginger, Garlic, and Siberian Ginseng.

USES: High and low blood pressure are both due to malfunctions of the circulatory system. These herbs can help stimulate that system, open the blood vessels, stabilize blood pressure, regulate hormones, and purify the circulatory system.

63.   CLEANSER PLUS CAPS
See #9

64.   FEMALE PROBLEMS

INGREDIENTS: Blessed Thistle, Golden Seal Root, Red Raspberry Leaves, Squaw Vine, Ginger, Cramp Bark, Capsicum, Uva Ursi, Marshmallow, Pan Pien Lien, and False Unicorn.

USES: Female problems include such conditions as endometriosis, cysts, tumors, menopause, and menstrual problems. This formula can help balance the body and provide nutrients to help promote healing.

65.   EXHAUSTION/ENERGY

INGREDIENTS: Siberian Ginseng, Gotu Kola, Bee Pollen, and Capsicum.

USES: This herbal formula is beneficial for increasing energy and fighting fatigue. This combination can help stimulate brain function. Surprisingly, it may also be used to ease the problems suffered during drug withdrawal .

66. HEART DISORDERS

INGREDIENTS: Hawthorn Berries, Capsicum, and Lecithin.

USES: This herbal combination has been found to be useful for problems of the circulatory system. It may help clear arteries suffering from arteriosclerosis, reduce cholesterol in the blood, and generally strengthen the condition of the heart.

67. INFECTION I (for people with low blood sugar)

INGREDIENTS: Echinacea, Myrrh Gum and Capsicum.

USES: This herbal combination is beneficial for building the immune system and preventing infection. It is especially useful for people suffering from low blood sugar. It may be of help with the lymph system, gangrene, and purulent infections.

68. INFECTION II

INGREDIENTS: Echinacea, Golden Seal Root, Burdock, Dandelion Root, and Capsicum.

USES: This formula can help with infections that invade the body by acting as a natural antibiotic, purifying the blood, building immunity and stimulating circulation. It is useful for infections such as tonsillitis, rheumatic fever, and intermittent infections.

69.   KIDNEY AND BLADDER

INGREDIENTS: Juniper Berries, Golden Seal Root, Parsley, Marshmallow, Watermelon Seeds, Uva Ursi, Pan Pien Lien, and Ginger.

USES: These herbs are beneficial in helping bedwetting, bladder infections, and kidney stones. The kidneys excrete urine which contains the end product of metabolism and help regulate bodily wastes, electrolytes and the acid/base content of the blood. This combination can help eliminate toxins in the kidneys, clear out obstructions, and soothe and help strengthen the urinary tract.

70.   LOWER BOWEL CLEANSER

INGREDIENTS: Cascara Sagrada, Barberry, Raspberry Leaves, Pan Pien Lien, Ginger, Rhubarb, Golden Seal Root, Fennel, and Cayenne.

USES: An underactive bowel can cause toxic wastes to be absorbed through the bowel wall and into the bloodstream. As toxins accumulate in the tissues, they can cause cell destruction. And this can lead to many ailments. This combination can help lower bowel problems by restoring tone to a relaxed bowel, removing matter from the bowel, strengthening the system, soothing the stomach, reducing inflammation, relieving gas and cramps and, in some cases, even eliminating bad breath in some people.

71. NERVOUSNESS I

INGREDIENTS: Valerian Root, Hops, Wood Betony, Scullcap, Black Cohosh, Mistletoe, Pan Pien Lien, Capsicum, and Lady's Slipper.

USES: This combination contains herbs beneficial for relaxation. It can help ease the tension accompanying an active life.

72. NERVOUSNESS II/ALLERGIES

INGREDIENTS: Valerian, Blessed Thistle, and Scullcap.

USES: This is another combination of herbs beneficial for relaxation. It can help ease the tension accompanying an active life.

73. PROSTATE PROBLEMS

INGREDIENTS: Golden Seal Root, Parsley, Marshmallow, Ginger, Capsicum, Queen of the Meadow, Juniper Berries, UvaUrsi, and Pan Pien Lien.

USES: This formula can play an important role in maintaining healthy prostate, bladder and kidney functions. It can help relieve inflammation, stop and clear infection, build tissue, and act as a natural diuretic.

74.   THYROID DISORDERS

INGREDIENTS: Norwegian Kelp, Irish Moss, Parsley, and Capsicum.

USES: The thyroid gland helps regulate metabolism. It is essential to many body functions. The herbs in the formula can help by promoting glandular health, controlling metabolism, purifying and strengthening cellular structure and stimulating blood circulation.

75.   ULCERS

INGREDIENTS: Golden Seal Root, Myrrh Gum, and Capsicum.

USES: This combination is beneficial for ulcers, canker sores, gum problems, pyorrhea, thrush and mouth cuts. These herbs aid as an internal disinfectant stopping infection, eliminating toxins from the stomach, and as an antiseptic promoting healing.

76.   VAGINAL CLEANSER

INGREDIENTS: Squaw Vine, Chickweed, Slippery Elm, Comfrey Root, Golden Seal Root, Yellow Dock, Mullein, and Marshmallow.

USES: This balance of herbs has been reported to help with vaginal problems as well as toxemia, cysts, polyps, and uterine tumors.

77.   WATER RETENTION

INGREDIENTS: Parsley, Marshmallow, Gravel Root, Ginger, Juniper Berries, Uva Ursi, Black Cohosh, Watermelon Seeds, and Pan Pien Lien.

USES: This combination of herbs can help relieve water retention and help with kidney and bladder problems.

78.   GINKGO COMBINATION

INGREDIENTS: Siberian Ginseng, Sage, Bee Pollen, Capsicum, and Ginkgo Biloba.

USES: This combination is very helpful for the entire body. It is used to increase circulation throughout the body. It is known to help with memory. It is also used to regulate blood pressure, increase endurance, relieve stress, increase longevity, and promote energy.

79.   ANTLER COMBINATION

INGREDIENTS: Elk Antler, Canadian Ginseng, Bee Pollen, Echinacea, Ginger, Cinnamon, and Capsicum.

USES: This unique combination is very beneficial for the immune system. It is thought to increase endurance and longevity. It is also used for sexual energy and as an aphrodisiac. It can help in cases of infection and with circulatory system problems.

HOMEOPATHIC FORMULAS

These combinations contain very small quantities of certain selected ingredients. These ingredients help the body avoid and heal disease.

80.   HAIR GROWTH/GLANDULAR

INGREDIENTS: Adrenals 4CH, Epiphyse 7CH, Hypophyse 7CH, Hypothalamus 7CH, Placenta 4CH, Thyroid 7CH, Silicea 8X, Spigelia CX, Corallium Rubrum 10X, Eleutherococcus 30X, Biotin 6X, and Graphites 4CH.

USES: This hair care treatment nourishes the body both internally and externally. This product seems to stimulate hair growth and nourishment. It aids in balancing the glandular system and increasing energy throughout the body.

81.   VISION CLARITY/CATARACTS

INGREDIENTS: Calcarea iodata 12X, Calcareafluorica
12X, Magnesia carbonica 8X, Naphta-
linum 6X, Vitamin A 12X, Euphrasia
6X, Julgans regia 6X, Cornea 7CH,
Pancreas 4CH, Ophtalmic Arteria 4CH,
Optic Nerve 7CH, and Liver 4CH.

USES: This formula was designed to improve the condition
of the eye. It can help with vision as well as cataracts.

82.   STOP SMOKING

INGREDIENTS: Spongia tosta 6X, Pulsatilla 6X, Hepar
sulphuris calcareum 8X, Bryonia alba
30X. Tabacum 6X, Nicotinum 8X,
Antimonium tartaricum 12X, Lobelia
inflata 6X, in 20% alcohol.

USES: This spray has been reported to help one cope with
nicotine withdrawal associated with quitting smoking.

HAIR CARE

Some hair and scalp problems are health-related. These formulas are designed to help maintain healthy hair and scalp.

83.   SHAMPOO

INGREDIENTS: Tea Tree Oil, Natural Polysaccharides, Panthenol (Vitamin B5), Tocopherol Acetate (Vitamin E), Biotin, and Wheat Germ Oil.

USES: This shampoo contains Tea Tree Oil for its soothing effect on the scalp. It stimulates the scalp but leaves no oily residue on the hair. It contains ingredients to add luster to the hair without drying it out.

84.   SHAMPOO SYSTEM

INGREDIENTS: See Hair Growth-Glandular and Shampoo.

USES: This product is a combination of the Hair Growth-Glandular (See #80, above) and Shampoo (See # 83, above).

EXTRACTS

These liquid extracts of single herbs or combinations of herbs are reported to be helpful for specific conditions. Certain ailments have been reported to respond better to extracts and some to encapsulated herbal products.

85. FLU AND EPIDEMICS

INGREDIENTS: Garlic, Gravel Root, Comfrey Root, Wormwood, Lobelia, Marshmallow, White Oak Bark, Black Walnut Hulls, Mullein Leaf, Scullcap, Uva Ursi, Apple Cider Vinegar, Glycerine, and Honey.

USES: This combination of herbal extracts is beneficial for the prevention and healing of many illnesses. It is believed to stimulate the immune system which may help protect the body from immune related diseases such as AIDS . It is also helpful in cases of the flu which spread rapidly.

86.   PARASITES

INGREDIENTS: Extract of Black Walnut Hulls in a base
                of Distilled Water and Ethyl Alcohol.
                High in organic iodine.

USES: Black Walnut has been reported to oxygenate the
blood which may help kill parasites and worms. This
extract can be helpful in healing poison oak, ringworm, and
other skin ailments.

87.   CIRCULATION

INGREDIENTS: Cayenne (Capsicum) in a base of
                Distilled Water and Ethyl Alcohol. High
                in Vitamin A, Vitamin C, Iron and
                Calcium.
USES: This extract is beneficial to the heart, circulatory
system, stomach and kidneys. It is considered a healer and
stimulates the body. It feeds and heals the cell structure of
the arteries, veins and capillaries. It is helpful in regulating
blood pressure. It may help stop bleeding both internally
and externally.

88.   HEMOGLOBIN BUILDER

INGREDIENTS: Chlorophyll derived from Alfalfa.
USES: The extract of chlorophyll derived from alfalfa has
many beneficial properties. It is useful for overall health and
strength. It can help clean the body, fight infection, deodorize
naturally, and soothe a sore throat. It is reported to be useful
for increasing milk production in nursing mothers .

89.   COLDS

INGREDIENTS: Peppermint, Elderberry, Sweet Orange Peel, Juniper Berry, Catnip, Marigold Flower, Angelica Root, White Pine Bark, Burdock, Peach Bark, Elecampane, Licorice, Honey, Glycerine, and Distilled Water.

USES: This herbal extract is beneficial in relieving the uncomfortable symptoms associated with colds and flu . It can relieve mucus and drain the sinuses. It is also useful for a sensitive stomach and digestive problems.

90.   COUGHS

INGREDIENTS: Chickweed, Licorice, Comfrey Root, Marshmallow, Mullein, Comfrey Leaf, Horehound, Lobelia, Cayenne, Distilled Water, and Glycerine.

USES: Often with a cold there is an irritating cough. This extract combination can soothe the tight and scratchy throat, relieve a hacking cough, and eliminate hoarseness.

91.   EXPECTORANT (Mucus)

INGREDIENTS: Garlic, Mullein, Comfrey Root, Fennel Seed, Comfrey Leaves, Lobelia, Distilled Water, Glycerine, and Apple Cider Vinegar.

USES: This extract formula can be helpful in loosening mucus. It can relieve congestion in bronchitis, pneumonia and emphysema.

92.   ANTIBIOTIC

INGREDIENTS: Golden Seal Root in a base of Distilled
                Water and Ethyl Alcohol.

USES: Golden Seal Root in an extract form is beneficial for
fighting infection as a natural antibiotic. It can also lower
blood sugar levels, clean the glands, and rid the body of
mucus.

93.   HEART

INGREDIENTS: Hawthorn Berries in a base of Glycerine
                and pure Grape Brandy.

USES: Hawthorn Berry has been used for centuries as
treatment for heart disease. This herbal extract is believed
to strengthen the heart muscles. It has been used in preventing arteriosclerosis. It is reported to help conditions
such as a rapid heart beat, weak heart, heart valve defects,
enlarged heart, angina pectoris, and difficulty in breathing
due to ineffective heart action and lack of oxygen in the
blood.

94.   NERVOUS SYSTEM

INGREDIENTS: Lady's Slipper in a base of Apple Cider
                Vinegar.

USES: This extract is excellent in relaxing the nervous system. It is useful for nervous tension, shingles, nervous
headaches, anxiety, shock and insomnia.

95. NERVOUSNESS

INGREDIENTS: Lobelia in a base of Apple Cider Vinegar.

USES: Lobelia is a relaxant. It has been reported helpful for all acute diseases. It is effective on the nerves, lungs, stomach, muscles, and circulatory system. It has healing powers to aid the entire body. It can remove congestion from the body and aid with respiratory problems such as allergies, mucus, bronchitis, and croup. It is beneficial in small doses to loosen mucus. It if helpful for childhood diseases, convulsions, headaches, and spasms.

96. COLD SORES

INGREDIENTS: Myrrh Gum in a base of Distilled Water and Ethyl Alcohol.

USES: Myrrh is a valuable herb as a cleansing and healing agent to the stomach and colon as it helps soothe inflammation and speed the healing process. It is a powerful antiseptic on the mucous membranes. The essential oils contain antiseptic properties and when mixed with water can be used as a gargle for sore throats. It is helpful for bad breath, bronchitis, chronic catarrh, hemorrhoids, lung disease, skin sores, and wounds. It is soothing and healing on cold sores.

97.   LOWER BOWEL CLEANSER

INGREDIENTS: Cascara Sagrada, Barberry, Raspberry
                  Leaves, Lobelia, Ginger, Rhubarb,
                  Golden Seal Root, Fennel and Cayenne.

USES: This formula is helpful in ridding the body of toxins. It also has a healing effect on the colon and especially
the lower bowel. It is useful for bad breath, diverticulitis,
and dysentery.

98.   PARASITES

INGREDIENTS: Black Walnut Hulls, Wormwood, Sage,
                  Fennel, Senna, Male Fern, Distilled
                  Water, and Glycerine.

USES: This herbal combination can be useful in killing
parasites in the body. It can help move waste material from
the body.

99.   BLOOD CLEANSER-CANCER

INGREDIENTS: Red Clover, Sheep Sorrel, Licorice Root,
                  Peach Bark, Barberry Root, Echinacea
                  Purpurea, Cascara Sagrada, Sarsaparil-
                  la, Prickly Ash Bark, Burdock Root,
                  Buckthorn, Rosemary Leaf, Distilled
                  Water, and Glycerine.

USES: This herbal extract formula is helpful for purifying the
blood and detoxifying poisons. It can help build the immune
system. Some believe it to be useful in fighting cancer, tumors,
mucus buildup, multiple sclerosis, and liver problems.

100. IMMUNE SYSTEM

INGREDIENTS: Extract of Taheebo (Pau d'Arco) bark.

USES: This formula is great for building the immune system. By strengthening the immune system, it is believed to help the body fight diseases such as AIDS, Candida, Diabetes, and Leukemia. A healthy immune system is the key to fighting all diseases.

101. ANTIFUNGAL OIL

INGREDIENTS: Tea Tree (Melaleuca) Oil.

USES: Tea Tree Oil is helpful in killing fungal growth. It can also be useful to heal staph infections and general skin disorders. It prevents infection, promotes healing, and acts as a local anesthetic to relieve pain.

102. MUSCLE SPASMS

INGREDIENTS: Scullcap, Myrrh Gum, Valerian Root, Skunk Cabbage, Lobelia, Black Cohosh Root, Capsicum, Distilled Water, and Alcohol.

USES: This combination of herbs in this extract are good for calming the body and relaxing the muscles. For this reason it may be helpful when muscles spasms occur. It may even be useful with epilepsy, lock jaw, convulsions, and a stiff neck.

103.   NERVOUSNESS

INGREDIENTS: Black Cohosh, Blue Cohosh, Blue Vervain, Scullcap, Lobelia, Distilled Water, and Alcohol.

USES: This extract has herbs which work together to soothe the nervous system. The nervous system is vital to life. And this combination can work as a mild sedative for the entire body and may relieve nervous tension. The drops have also been used to stop ringing in the ears.

104.   CONGESTION

INGREDIENTS: Hyssop in a base of Distilled Water and Glycerine.

USES: Hyssop is useful for lung ailments and congestion problems. It is used for fevers because it can help produce sweating. It contains essential hormones to build resistance to infectious disease. It has been used for poor digestion, breast and lung problems, coughs from colds and nose and throat infections. It is useful for mucus congestion in the intestines. It can be used externally to relieve muscular aches, pains and bruises.

VITAMINS AND SUPPLEMENTS

While most often found in popular multi-vitamin pills, vitamins and other nutritional supplements are more effective when taken in their more natural state.

105.   ACIDOPHILUS

INGREDIENTS: Freeze-dried Lactobacillus Acidophilus culture in a non-dairy base.

USES: Acidophilus can help increase the amount of friendly bacteria in the colon which are essential for proper digestion and the production of B vitamins. It can help strengthen the immune system and reduce toxic waste in the large intestine. Acidophilus has been reported helpful in cases of Candida.

106.   B-COMPLEX (Yeast Free)

INGREDIENTS: B-Vitamins in a base of Rice Bran, Bee
                Pollen and Kelp.

USES: The B-Complex vitamins are needed daily by the
body. They are helpful for the entire nervous system and
can aid in controlling stress. They also promote a healthy
digestive tract. They help with appetite stimulation, digestion, assimilation and elimination. They assist enzymes in
metabolism of proteins, fats and carbohydrates. The B vitamins help sustain normal function of the gastrointestinal
tract. They also help prevent and treat canker sores in the
mouth.

107.   CALCIUM COMBINATION

INGREDIENTS: Calcium and Magnesium [from B o n e
                Meal, Oyster Shell, Magnesium Oxide,
                Betaine HCL (hydrochloric acid)],
                Vitamins B1, B2, and D in a Comfrey
                Root, Alfalfa, and Kelp base.

USES: Calcium is essential for smooth functioning of the
heart muscles. It is important for the proper formation of
bones and teeth. It also aids in the muscular movement of
the intestines which help with the digestion process. And
this calcium combination aids in the absorption of calcium,
so the body can assimilate it more efficiently.

108. VITAMIN C

INGREDIENTS: Vitamin C, Citrus Bioflavonoids, Hesperidin Complex, Rutin, Rose Hips, and Acerola.

USES: Vitamin C is useful in preventing infection by increasing and speeding up activity of the white blood cells and destroying viruses and bacteria. It is essential to glandular activity and defending the body against harmful substances in the environment. Vitamin C also helps form collagen which is important for teeth and bones.

109. VITAMIN E

INGREDIENTS: 100% natural mixed Tocopherols in a base of Natural Wheat Germ Oil and Lecithin.

USES: Vitamin E is an important antioxidant. It is reported to enhance oxygenation of blood, reduce cholesterol, increase fertility and male potency, and revitalize and strengthen the heart muscles. It may also be useful in healing and preventing scarring of the skin.

110. COQ10

INGREDIENTS: CoQ10, Hawthorn Concentrated Extract and Powder, Cayenne, and Herbal Oils.

USES: This combination is designed to be very helpful for the heart. It may help stop chest pains as in angina pectoris. It may also help with mitral valve prolapse, and high blood pressure. It has been reported to be useful in oxygenating the tissue and cells of the body and in healing gum disease, diabetes, and increasing energy.

111. IRON

INGREDIENTS: Iron Fumerate, Copper Gluconate,
Vitamin B-12, Folic Acid and Yellow
Dock in an herbal base of Dandelion
Root and Kelp.

USES: Iron is very useful for individuals who suffer from
anemia. The ingredients in this combination can help with
the absorption of iron. It is useful in protein metabolism,
oxygenating the lungs and cells, improving circulation,
increasing mental vitality, liver and kidney function, and
digestion and elimination.

112. POTASSIUM

INGREDIENTS: Potassium Gluconate in a base of Kelp,
Alfalfa, and Parsley.

USES: Potassium helps regulate the water balance in the
body. It assists in repairing cells of the body and is considered a healing mineral.

113. DIGESTION

INGREDIENTS: Pancreatin, N.F., Pepsin, Papain,
Bromelain, Ox Bile, Betaine Hydrochlo-
ride in a base of Peppermint Leaves,
Comfrey and Slippery Elm.

USES: This supplement may be helpful with digestive
problems. It helps assimilate food so nutrients are more
easily absorbed by the body.

114.   LECITHIN

INGREDIENTS: Lecithin derived from Soybeans.

USES: Lecithin is reported to be helpful in heart regula-
tion, reducing cholesterol and in overall cardiovascular
health. It helps by breaking down fat and cholesterol and
inhibiting them from adhering to the artery walls. It helps
fight infection and increase resistance to disease.

115.   CIRCULATION

INGREDIENTS: Chelated Vitamins, Minerals, Amino
Acids, Glandulars, Herbs and Essential
Fatty Acids.

USES: This combination is helpful in increasing circulation
in the body systems. It can help in eliminating toxic metals
in the body, lowering cholesterol levels, and reducing
hypertension.

116.   LIQUID MINERALS (concentrated)

INGREDIENTS: Contains six macro-minerals and seven-
ty micro-minerals from sea water.

USES: Minerals are essential for all body functions. These
are easily assimilated trace minerals that have been broken
down for the body to utilize. Mineral balance is essential
to the body chemistry.

117.   SALMON OIL

INGREDIENTS: Fatty Acids (EPA and DHA), naturally
                contained in Salmon Omega-3 Oil.

USES: This combination is believed to be useful in lowering cholesterol, preventing arteriosclerosis and healing
psoriasis.

118.   GERMANIUM

INGREDIENTS: Germanium and Odorless Garlic.

USES: This product is helpful in relieving pain, building
the body's immune system, and improving circulation
throughout the body.

OINTMENTS

Ointments are herbs and herbal combinations combined in a manner to be used externally.

119. BONE/MUSCLE/CARTILAGE OINTMENT

INGREDIENTS: White Oak Bark, Comfrey Root, Wormwood, Lobelia, Scullcap, Black Walnut Hulls, Queen of the Meadow, Marshmallow, Mullein, in a base of cold pressed Olive Oil, Tallow, and Beeswax.

USES: This ointment is beneficial when used on external injuries. It can be helpful when applied to sprains, strains, bruises, and sore joints.

120.   SKIN IRRITATION

INGREDIENTS: Golden Seal Root, Myrrh, Comfrey Root, St. John's Wort, Plantain, Chickweed, Wintergreen, Sage, Gum Benzoin, Olive Oil, and Beeswax.

USES: This ointment is helpful in healing and soothing skin irritations and abrasions. It can help stop and prevent infections on the skin surface.

121.   SUNBURNS/CUTS/RASHES

INGREDIENTS: Irish Moss Tea, Lecithin, Aloe Vera Juice, Almond Oil, Cocoa Butter, Oil of Myrrh Gum, Fir Needle, Nutmeg, Rosemary, and Wintergreen.

USES: This combination of natural products is soothing and promotes healing when applied to blisters, sore muscles, minor sunburn, bruises, muscle cramps, sprains, rashes, eczema, insect bites, and tension headaches.

122.   BURNS

INGREDIENTS: Comfrey Root, Marshmallow Root, Marigold (Calendula), Malva, Chickweed, Mullein, Plantain, Pepper-mint Oil, Olive Oil, and Tallow.

USES: This combination ointment is helpful with minor injuries such as cuts, scrapes, abrasions, and skin irritations from poisonous plants such as poison ivy, sumac, and stinging nettle.

SINGLE HERBS

These herbs are listed alphabetically and an explanation is given as to historical uses and reported effects of using these herbs.

123. ALFALFA (Medicago sativa)

Alfalfa assists in digestion and assimilation of nutrients in the body. It contains eight essential digestive enzymes. It provides essential minerals, vitamins and enzymes to nourish and strengthen the body. Alfalfa helps to eliminate uric acid which eases arthritis problems. It is rich in protein and contains tryptophan which helps to relax the nerves. Alfalfa contains alkaloid in the leaves which strengthen the central nervous system. It is useful for chemical imbalance, cleaning the blood in cases of toxemia, helping prevent cholesterol accumulation in the veins and in cleaning, building and strengthening the entire body.

124. ALOE VERA (Aloe vera)

Aloe Vera is a very useful herb. It is helpful on the skin when applied to scars, scalds, burns, and itchy skin irritations. It can relieve pain on contact because it contains salicylic acid and magnesium which work together directly on burns as an aspirin-like analgesic. It can clean the stomach, colon and entire system. Aloe Vera contains glycoside aloin which stimulates the colon and eliminates toxins. It can help with cholesterol buildup, throat problems, hiatal hernia, intestinal problems, chronic constipation, acid stomach, ulcers, and gastritis.

125.   BEE POLLEN

Bee Pollen is high in protein and is considered to be a complete food. It contains rich sources of vitamins, minerals, protein, amino acids, hormones, enzymes and fats. It can help when there is a hormone imbalance in the body. It is useful in cases of hypertension and nervous and endocrine system disorders. It increases energy and mental alertness. It can help build the body to resist disease and increase the healing power of the body. It is also believed to be useful in slowing down the aging process and retaining youthful energy. Bee Pollen has helped those with allergies and hayfever to build up immunity. It can help improve appetite, normalize intestinal activity, strengthen capillary walls, offset effects of drugs and pollutants, heal colitis, and improve anemia.

126.   BLACK COHOSH (Cimicifuga racemosa)

This herb is useful in equalizing blood circulation throughout the body. It can help with the heart and lungs to strengthen them. It can aid the uterus and may be used in the last weeks of pregnancy to strengthen and stimulate uterine contractions in childbirth. Black Cohosh is also believed to stimulate natural estrogen production and many women benefit from its use during menopause instead of resorting to estrogen supplements. It is effective in balancing the hormones. It acts directly on the spinal nerves as a relaxant. It is able to loosen and expel mucus from the bronchial tubes.

127.   BLACK WALNUT (Juglans nigra)

Black Walnut is beneficial for the blood, intestines, and nerves. It contains rich organic iodine and tannins which contain antiseptic properties. It is excellent for killing para- sites and worms in the body. It has oxygenating abilities which burn up excess toxins and fatty materials. It can help to regulate blood sugar levels in the body. Black Walnut contains natural flouride which can strengthen teeth. It can be used externally on skin problems such as athlete's foot to heal and sooth.

128.   BLUE VERVAIN (Verbena hastata)

Blue Vervain is considered a tonic herb. It has been use effectively as an expectorant, antispasmodic, and sudorifc. It strengthens the body to heal diseases of the liver and spleen. It works in cases of viral colds and fevers to ease and soothe. It can help to stimulate suppressed menstrua- tion. It can increase the circulation in the body. It is effective in hysteria, epilepsy, palsy, nervous exhaustion, hallucina- tions, coughs, earaches, headaches, diarrhea, insomnia, and dysentery. It can settle the stomach and produce an overall relaxed feeling of well-being.

129.   BURDOCK (Arctium lappa)

This herb is an excellent blood cleanser to eliminate uric acid and excess waste material. It contains mucilage which contains antifungal and anti-bacterial properties.It can aid in neutralizing toxins in the blood. It acts on the pituitary gland to help adjust hormone imbalances, and also soothes the hypothalamus. Burdock is believed to eliminate congestion from the lymphatic system. It has been used to help eliminate calcification in the joints and prevent it from accumulating.

130.   CAYENNE (Capsicum frutescens)

Cayenne works on the heart, circulation, stomach and kidneys. It is a healer. It appears to work by stimulating the whole body which helps healing to take place. It feeds and heals the cell structure of arteries, veins and capillaries. It is reported to help regulate blood pressure. It is believed to stop bleeding both internally and externally. As a result, it may help stop heart attacks, strokes, colds, flu, low vitality, headaches, indigestion, depression, arthritis, and ulcers.

131.   CASCARA SAGRADA (Rhamnus purshiana)

This herb is reported to be very helpful for chronic constipation. It is considered one of the best and safest laxatives in the herbal kingdom. It can restore tone to the relaxed bowel and help with most digestive complaints. It is beneficial for most illnesses because of its ability to cleanse the bowels. It is believed to increase secretions of the liver, lower bowel, pancreas, and stomach. It has an antibiotic effect on harmful bacteria in the intestines. Cascara Sagrada may also help with insomnia, high blood pressure, hemorrhoids, and liver and gallbladder problems.

132.   DEVIL'S CLAW (Harpagophytum procumbens)

This is an herb that is said to be beneficial on the liver, joints, kidneys, and stomach. It has been used successfully to relieve arthritis, gout, and rheumatism. Devil's Claw acts as a blood and vascular wall cleanser. It is a natural cleanser used to eliminate toxins from the lymph glands and system.

133.   DONG QUAI (Angelica sinensis)

Dong Quai is said to be very effective as an herb for female problems. It has a tranquilizing effect on the central nervous system and gives nourishment to the brain cells. It nourishes blood, lubricates the intestines, and promotes growth of the womb. It may help with cramps, irregular menstruation, hot flashes, and menopausal symptoms. It possesses nourishment for female glands and helps strengthen all internal body organs and muscles. As a result, it has been used to help rebuild the blood and improve the condition of pregnant women. It may help dissolve blood clots, loosen tight muscles, cleanse and purify the blood and help increase circulation. Dong Quai is also said to be useful in dissolving blood clots, relieving low blood sugar and high blood pressure and help with internal bleeding and bruising.

134.   ECHINACEA (Echinacea augustifolia)

Echinacea helps to stimulate the immune response of the body and helps increase the body's ability to resist infection. It has the ability to promote production of white blood cells. It is helpful as a blood purifier. It improves lymphatic filtration and drainage and helps remove toxins from the body. It is effective against bacterial and viral infections and is considered a natural antibiotic. It is used in cases involving abscesses, gangrene, pus, swollen lymph glands and infections. It has been used for blood poisoning, snake and spider bites .

135.   GINGER (Zingiber officinale)

Ginger is effective for nausea, sea sickness, and flu symptoms. It can calm and soothe the stomach to alleviate stomach cramps. It prevents cramping when used in combination with laxative herbs. It has been used to relieve upset stomachs and indigestion. It is used as a cleansing agent of the bowels, kidneys, and skin. Ginger is also used for respiratory systems. It is reported to be helpful in fighting off colds and flu by removing congestion and relieving headaches, aches and pains. It is also said to be used with other herbs to enhance their effectiveness.

136.   GINSENG, SIBERIAN (Eleutherococcus)

Ginseng is used extensively in the Orient. It is used there to stimulate the entire body to increase energy and overcome stress, fatigue, and weakness. It is stimulating for mental fatigue and improving brain cells. It has a beneficial effect on the heart and circulation. It is used to normalize blood pressure, reduce blood cholesterol and prevent arteriosclerosis. Some use it to slow the aging process. It acts as an antidote to some drugs, toxic chemicals, and protects the body against radiation. It is reported to be a great preventive herb for disease and beneficial in restoring health and rejuvenation after illness. It may improve concentration and increase speed and accuracy in work.

137.   GOLDEN SEAL ROOT (Hydrastis canadensis)

This herb is reported to act as a natural antibiotic to stop infection and kill poisons in the body. Golden Seal may boost a sluggish glandular system and promote hormone production. The herb goes directly into the bloodstream and helps regulate liver function. Golden Seal also is reported to act as natural insulin by providing the body with nutrients necessary to produce its own insulin. It helps to regulate blood sugar. It stops internal and external bleeding. It is healing to the mucous membranes and helps eliminate toxins in the body.

138.   GOTU KOLA (Hydrocotyle asiatica)

Gotu Kola is useful as a brain food to rebuild energy reserves and stamina. It can increase mental and physical power. It combats stress and improves reflexes. It is known to relieve high blood pressure. It is said to be a valuable treatment for depression and mental problems by helping with mental fatigue, senility, schizophrenia, epilepsy, and memory loss. It neutralizes blood toxins and helps balance hormones and relax the nerves.

139.   HAWTHORN BERRIES (Crategnus oxyacantha)

Hawthorn Berries are very effective for relieving insomnia. They are useful for heart disease. They are reported to help improve a feeble heart, valvular insufficiency, a pulse irregularity, an enlarged heart, arteriosclerosis, and angina pectoris. They may also help with breathing problems due to ineffective heart action and lack of oxygen in the blood. They may help regulate blood pressure whether high or low. They are said to be excellent for the nerves and helpful for hypoglycemia.

140.   HORSETAIL (Equisetum arvense)

This herb is a healer and builder of bones, flesh, cartilage, and teeth. It is rich in silicon which is essential in calcium metabolism. It is a healer for problems of athletes such as broken bones, stretched ligaments, discs, tendons, and for strengthening the skeleton to prevent injuries. It is also used for urinary tract disorders and to help with urine retention, kidney stones and problems, and eye and skin disorders. Horsetail is reported to aid in coagulation and to help decrease bleeding. It contains the ingredient silicic acid which is said to help aid circulation.

141.   HO SHOU WU (Polygonum multiflorum)

Ho Shou Wu is a member of the Smartweed family. It has a toning effect on the liver and kidneys. It is beneficial for the nervous system and is used as a tonic for endocrine glands. It is said to be helpful for the brain and memory. It is also said to promote female hormone function, improve health, and increase stamina and resistance to disease. It may help dilate blood vessels which can aid in the healing of traumatic bruises. It is also reported to be helpful for pre- mature graying of hair, backaches, aches and pains of the knee joints and neurasthenia.

142.   HYDRANGEA (Hydrangea arborescens)

Hydrangea is an herb with many curative properties. It contains alkaloids that act like cortisone helping to reduce inflammation. It may also help prevent gravel deposits in the kidneys and gall bladder. It is said to help relieve pain when stones pass through the urethra from the kidneys to the bladder. It may help relieve an inflamed or enlarged prostate gland. It is reported to be beneficial for arthritis, bladder infections, cystitis, gallstones, gout, kidney prob- lems and urinary problems.

143.   KELP, NORWEGIAN (Fucus visiculosis)

Kelp is beneficial to the body because it contains about thirty trace and major minerals. These help the body to eliminate waste and toxic metals, regulate metabolism, and help glands to function properly. It is helpful to relieve ner- vous disorders and prevent hair loss. It is reported to strengthen tissues in the brain and heart. Kelp has the rep- utation of speeding up the burning of excess calories by controlling the body's metabolism and is helpful in the nourishment of the body.

144.   LICORICE (Glycyrrhiza glabra)

Licorice is a source of the female hormone estrogen. It stimulates the body to produce its own natural estrogen and cortisone which are helpful for female disorders. It is also reported to stimulate the adrenal glands. Licorice contains glycosides which can chemically purge excess fluid from the lungs, throat and body. Thus, it is said to be useful for coughs and chest complaints. It is helpful when recovering from illness and will help supply energy to the body. It also works as a laxative and helps with inflammation of the intestinal tract and ulcers. It has a stimulating action which helps counteract stress. It is useful for colds, flu, coughs, and lung congestion. It is also reported to help voice muscles and heal hoarseness and throat damage.

145.   LOBELIA (Pan Pien Lien)

Lobelia is said to be excellent for all acute diseases. It is a relaxant. It is said to help remove obstruction from any part of the body. It has no known harmful side effects. It is said to help remove congestion within the body especially the blood vessels. Lobelia is also helpful for bronchial spasms. It may be able to help clear up allergies, asthma, bronchitis, childhood diseases, convulsions, croup, headaches, and spasms.

146.   PASSION FLOWER (Passiflora incarnata)

Passion Flower is an herb with properties helpful for the nerves and circulation. It is high in calcium which strengthens the nervous system. It is said to be good for nervousness, agitation, exhaustion and insomnia. It is also relaxing for coughs, colds, convulsions, hysteria, muscle twitching, and irritability. It is sais to useful for inflamed eyes and dimness of vision. It is excellent for all acute diseases. It is also helpful for fevers, menopause pain, and headaches .

147.   PAU D'ARCO (Tabebuia avellanedae)

Pau d'Arco is reported to be a natural blood cleanser and builder. It has antibiotic properties which can aid in destroying viral infections in the body. It has been used to give the body strength and energy and to protect and strengthen the immune system. It has been said to be helpful in combating cancer. It has been used in healing diseases such as arthritis, asthma, diabetes, gonorrhea, hemorrhage, hernia, infection, liver ailments, lupus, Parkinson's disease, pyorrhea, skin problems, spleen, ulcers, varicose veins, and wounds.

148.   PSYLLIUM (Plantago ovata)

Psyllium is considered a colon and intestine cleanser. It lubricates as well as heals the intestines and colon. It does not irritate the mucous membranes of the intestines but strengthens the tissues and restores tone. It absorbs acids and toxins in the intestinal tract. It is reported to be good for auto-intoxication, which can cause many diseases, by cleansing the intestines and removing toxins. It creates bulk and fiber which is lacking in the typical American diet. It is considered a food and may be used daily for healthy bowels.

149.   RED RASPBERRY (Rubys idaeus)

This herb is used to help with the common cold, flu, and fevers. It is also used for stomach pain and diarrhea. It is reported to have properties helpful for women, especially during pregnancy. It contains nutrients which strengthen the uterine wall and reproductive system. It is said to help relieve nausea, prevent hemorrhaging, reduce pain and ease childbirth. It is reported to help reduce false labor pains. It is also said to help enrich colostrum found in breast milk. Red Raspberry has also been used to help children with colds, colic, and fevers.

150. SAFFRON (Crocus satirus)

This herb is believed to be beneficial in strengthening the heart and preventing heart disease. It is also said to soothe the membranes of the stomach and colon . It is also said to help reduce cholesterol levels by neutralizing uric-acid build-up in the blood. Saffron, when dissolved in hot water, causes perspiration and helps to reduce fever and relieve pain in cases of measles, mumps, and chicken pox. It is also said to help digest protein and fat in the diet. It is an aid to digestion and is reported to be helpful in cases of gas, heartburn, insomnia, stomach disorders and water retention.

151. SLIPPERY ELM (Ulmus fulva)

This nutritious herb is used both internally and externally for healing. It is reported to have beneficial effects throughout the whole body. Slippery Elm has been used to neutralize stomach acidity. It aids in the digestion of milk. It is used as a buffer against irritations and inflammations of the mucous membranes. It helps assist the activity of the adrenal glands. It helps boost the output of cortin hormone which helps send a stream of blood-building substances through the cardiovascular system. It is said to draw out impurities and heal all parts of the body. It has been used as a remedy for the respiratory system by removing mucus from the body. It heals and soothes inflamed or irritated areas of the body. It is equal to oatmeal in vitamin and mineral content. It is reported to be helpful for bronchitis, colitis, croup, and urinary and bowel problems.

152.   SUMA (Pfaffia paniculate martius)

Suma is called "Brazilian Ginseng" by some herbalists. It has been used as a tonic, aphrodisiac (increasing well-being), for skin problems, diabetes and tumors. It contains germanium, a trace mineral which is said to stimulate the immune system and help oxygen flow to the cells. It also is reported to help balance estrogen levels as well as decrease high blood cholesterol. It contains allantoin (like comfrey) which is used to promote wound healing. It also contains essential vitamins, minerals and amino acids.

153.   VALERIAN (Valeriana officinalis)

Valerian is considered a nervine herb and may be helpful for insomnia. It contains essential oils and alkaloids which reportedly combine to produce a calming, sedative effect. Thus, it is used as a safe, non-narcotic herbal sedative and has been used in cases of anxiety. This nourishing and soothing effect has been reported to help reduce tension, hysteria and stress. It is said to be calming for all nervous disorders. It has been used for after-pains in childbirth, arthritis, cramps, headaches, heart palpitations and muscle spasms.

154.   WHITE OAK BARK (Quercus alba)

White Oak Bark contains strong astringent properties
that can be used both internally and externally. It has been
used as a cleanser for inflamed areas of the skin and
mucous membranes such as vaginal infections, piles, hemorrhoids, and varicose veins . It has been used to heal damaged tissues in the stomach and intestines. It has been used
for excess stomach mucus which is a common complaint of
individuals suffering from sinus congestion and post-
nasal drip. It relieves the stomach by strengthening it per-
mitting better internal absorption and secretion and
improving its metabolism. It has been reported to stop
hemorrhaging in the intestines, bowels, lungs and kidneys.
It has also been used to heal gums, as an antiseptic for
sores, as a gargle for thrush, and for tonsillitis and mouth
ulcers. It has also been used to help heal yeast infections.

155.   WILD YAM (Dioscorea villosa)

Wild Yam has been used to help treat nausea in pregnant women. It is also said to help prevent miscarriage. It
has also been used for cramps which occur during the later
stages of pregnancy as it is helpful for reliving abdominal
cramps and bowel spasms. It relaxes the muscular fibers,
soothes the nerves and helps relieve pain. It has been val-
ued as an herb to help nervousness, restlessness, and nausea.

SKIN CARE

The skin is an important part of total body health. With the toxic environment in which we live, skin care is even more important. These products can help the skin and protect it from the damaging effects of the world in which we live.

156.   PROTECTANT AND MOISTURIZER

INGREDIENTS: Deionized Water, Propane/Isobutane, Pyrrolidinone, Dimethicone, Stearic Acid, Myristic Acid, Ceteareth 20, Cetearyl Alcohol, Aloe Vera Gel, Isopropyl Myristate, Cetyl Alcohol, Glycerin, Nonoxynol 9, Propylene Glycol, Oxaban E, Vitamin E (Tocopheryl Acetate), Fragrance, Triethanolamine, Hexetidine.

USES: This natural product is an all-purpose skin protectant and moisturizer. It acts as an extra layer of skin between the skin and the environment. It blocks out harmful contaminants, skin irritants, harsh detergents, and chemicals. It helps shield against germs, bacteria, and odors. It also helps the skin retain its own moisture.

157.   SUNSCREEN

INGREDIENTS: Aloe Vera Concentrate, Deionized Water, Titanium Dioxide, Isopropyl Myristate, TEA-Stearate, Glycerin, Isopropyl Palmitate, Cetearyl Alcohol, Ceteareth 20, Petrolatum, Cetyl Alcohol, PVP, Dimethicone, Propylene Glycol, Live Yeast Cell Derivative, Nonoxynol-9, Hexetidine, 7-Ethyl Bicyclooxazolidine, Methylparaben, Tocophero, Fragrance,   Imidazolidinyl Urea, Propylparaben.

USES: Exposure to the sun can cause permanent damage to the skin. This product is helpful in screening the skin from the damaging effects of the sun's rays.

158.   BODY SCRUB

INGREDIENTS: Aloe Vera Concentrate, Deionized Water, TEA-Stearate, Glyceryl Stearate, PEG-100 Stearate, Almond Meal, Titanium   Dioxide,   Petrolatum, Propylene Glycol, Panthenol, Allantoin, Cetyl   Alcohol,   Sodium   PCA, Polysorbate-80, Lactic Acid, Methylparaben, Fragrance, Imidazolidinyl Urea, Propylparaben, Ascorbic Acid, Tocopherol .

USES: This natural body cleansing product is gentle on the skin. It cleanses the skin to remove dirt, bacteria and oils from the skin.

159. SUNLESS TAN

INGREDIENTS: Aloe Vera Concentrate, Deionized Water, Dihydroxyacetone, Glycerin, Cetearyl Alcohol, Ceteareth-20, Glyceryl Stearate, Jojoba Oil, Allantoin, Sodium PCA, Panthenol, Hydrolyzed Mucopolysaccharide, Squalene, Cetyl Alcohol, Dimethicone, Isopropyl Palmitate, Tocopherol, Methylparaben, Fragrance, Propylparaben, Retinol, Ergocalciferol .

USES: Many desire the look of tanning. But since the sun may damage the skin, this product can help produce a natural looking tan without the sun. It also moisturizes the skin.

160. TAN SAVER

INGREDIENTS: Aloe Vera Concentrate, Deionized Water, Benzethonium Chloride, Allantoin, Hydrolyzed Mucopolysaccharides, Sodium PCA, Methylparaben, Imidazolidinyl Urea, Propylparaben.

USES: The tan saver can help the skin retain a tan. It also works to moisturize the skin.

161.   MINERAL MIST

INGREDIENTS: Ora Water.

USES: This natural product is useful for moisturizing, soothing and protecting the skin.

162.   NATIVE MASQUE

INGREDIENTS: Ora Water, Tropical Seaplant.

USES: The native masque can help rejuvenate and soften the skin. It brings a soften and youthful appearance to the skin.

SKIN REVIVING PRODUCTS

These natural products are not considered skin care but a totally new approach to treating the skin. Studies have been done in major universities and laboratories throughout the world using alphahydroxy acids (AHAs). AHAs are naturally occuring, non-toxic substances found in sour milk, grapes, citrus fruits, apples and sugar cane. They have been found to reduce some of the visible signs of aging by removing the dry, dead cells that dull the skin's surface, while simultaneously improving the overall integrity and texture of the complexion. The Skin Reviving products replace the traditional steps with at new approach; first, exfoliating and cleansing the skin, second, protecting the skin from the sun and elements, and third, repairing and nourishing the skin.

The skin needs to be treated like the living, breathing organ that it is and not suffocated and plumped up with surface emollients and ingredients such as collagen, elastin, or placental extracts that make the skin appear smoother. These products assist the skin in becoming healthy naturally.

163.   EXFOLIANT

INGREDIENTS: Almond Glycerides, Beta -1, 3-Glucan, Cocamide DEA, Glucose Polymer, Glycolic Polymer, Glycoprotein, Succinate, Essential Oils and others.

USES: This is the first step of this skin program. It helps clear the skin of dull, dead cells each morning.

164.   TONER

INGREDIENTS: Ascorbate, Carotenoids, Glutathione, Uric Acid, Witch Hazel, Essential Oils and others.

USES: The toner helps protect the skin from environmental damage.

165.   REPAIR I

INGREDIENTS: Aloe Vera, EGF (Epidermal Growth Factor), Essential Oils, Glycerol Stearate, Lecithin, Pumpkin Oil, Retinyl Palmitate, Sunflower/Safflower, Tocopheryl Acetate and others.

USES: This product can help the skin naturally recover from damaged caused by the environment.

166.   CLEANSER

INGREDIENTS: Alpha Glucan, Beta-1, 3-Glucan, Chitin, Cocamide DEA, Essential Oils, Glucose Polymer, Glycoprotein, Witch Hazel, and others.

USES: This cleanser is a new approach. It encourages the skin to reject epidermal metabolic waste and environmental impurities.

167.   NIGHT LOTION

INGREDIENTS: Allantoin, Almond Oil, Beta-1, 3-Glucan, Essential Oils, Glycerol Stearate, Glycolic Polymer, Glycoprotein, Lecithin, Olive Oil, Retinyl Palmitate, Sunflower / Safflower, Tocopheryl Acetate , and others.

USES: This works overnight to gently exfoliate and feed the new cells with nutrients to help restore the skin 's own repair mechanisms.

168.   FIRMING LOTION

INGREDIENTS: Birch, Cypress, EGF (Epidermal Growth Factor), Essential Oils, Fennel, Grapefruit, Juniper, Pumpkin Oil, Red Thyme, and others.

USES: This can be used on the skin around the hips and thighs to help firm and tone.

169.   REPAIR II

INGREDIENTS: Beta-1, 3-Glucan, Essential Oils, Glycoprotein, Lactic Acid Polymer, Lemon Extract, Milk Protein, Olive Oil, Sunflower / Safflower, and others.

USES: This is formulated to be used under the eyes to firm and repair the fine lines that appear from damage and aging.

OTHER ITEMS

170.   NATURAL SELECT

INGREDIENTS: Whey, Corn Syrup Solids, Whey Protein
Concentrate, High Oleic Sunflower Oil,
Calcium Carbonate, Modified Food
Starch, Tri-Calcium Phosphate, Calcium
Sulfate, Natural and Artificial Flavors,
Soy Lecithin, Dipotassium Phosphate,
Mono and Diglycerides.

USES: This product is a milk substitute rich in calcium and
easily assimilated by the body. It is a nutritious drink to be
used any time of the day. It is great for cooking and drink-
ing. It offers the benefits of animal protein from low-fat
whey instead of plant proteins.

171.   NATURAL SELECT (Chocolate) (See #168)

172.   FIBER SUPPLEMENT

INGREDIENTS: Psyllium Husk, Fructose, Maltodextrin, Fructooligo Saccharide, Citrus Pectin, Natural Orange Flavor, Hisbiscus Flower, Natural Banana Flavor, Guar Gum, Caa Inhem Extract, Peppermint Leaf Powder, Cinnamon Bark Powder, Papaya Fruit Powder, Garlic Powder, Rhubarb Root Powder, Alfalfa Powder, Fenugreek Seed Powder, Slippery Elm Bark Powder, Ginger Root Powder, Cape Aloe, Burdock Root Powder, Black Walnut Hulls Powder, Red Raspberry Leaf Powder, Pumpkin Seed Powder, Yucca Root Powder, Marshmallow Root (Althea), Uva Ursi Powder, Buchu Leaf Powder, Capsicum Fruit Powder, Clove Seed Powder, Chickweed Powder, Cornsilk Powder, Dandelion Root Powder, Echinacea Root Powder (Augustifolia), and False Unicorn.

USES: Add the powder to water, juice or other beverages. There has been much research done as to the benefits of a high fiber diet. This product can help put fiber in the diet that is missing from the food that we eat. It contains two kinds of fiber; both insoluble and soluble. The insoluble fiber passes through the system without dissolving in water. Its bulk helps make digestion cleaner and faster. Soluble fiber dissolves in water and may, with the help of a low fat diet, lower blood cholesterol levels.

173. HEART PLUS

INGREDIENTS: Vitamin A, Vitamin C, Niacin, Vitamin E, Folic Acid, Vitamin B 12, Magnesium, Zinc, Selenium, Potassium, White Willow Bark, Deodorized Garlic, Hawthorne Berry Concentrate, Ginkgo Biloba Concentrate, Coenzyme Q10, and L-Carnitine.

USES: This combination is beneficial to the circulatory system. It helps guard the arteries and heart against damage from free radicals. It can help reduce low density lipid forms of cholesterol and improve blood flow.

174. MEN'S FORMULA

INGREDIENTS: Dehydrated Broccoli Concentrate, Zinc Proteinate, Serenoa Repens Concentrate and Beta-Carotene.

USES: This formula is designed for the nutritonal needs of men. It is useful for healthy skin, nails and male virility. It also promotes male hormone balance.

175. WOMEN'S FORMULA

INGREDIENTS: Dehydrated Broccoli Concentrate in a clear gelatin capsule.

USES: This formula is designed to supplement the female body with a nuritional blend of concentrated cruciferous vegetable. These have been found valuable as reducing the risk of cancer including breast cancer. It is also known to help with female hormone balance.

176. CALM

INGREDIENTS: Fluid extract of Skullcap, Passiflora, Wild Yam Root and Valerian Root in a Sorbitol Base.

USES: This extract is beneifical for ailments involving the nervous system. It has a soothing effect on the nerves . It contains alkaloids which posess sedative and muscle relax-ant properties. It can be used for insomnia, restlessness, hysteria, and nervous headache.

177. DIGESTION

INGREDIENTS: Psyllium Seed Husk, Rice Bran, and a yogurt culture.

USES: This formula helps promote regulatrity in the body. It can help assist the body in elimination when constipation is a problem. It may help lower the risk of colon cancer and cardivascular disorder. It may help lower cholesterol levels by binding bile acids. It can help in the digestion process.

178. HERBAL SUPPORT

INGREDIENTS: Extracts of Angelica Root, Buckthorn Bar, Horehound Herb, Parsley Seeds, Cassica Leaves, Bitterroot, Sweet Wood Rootstock, Thyme Herb, White Endive Plant, Saw Palmetto Berries, Milk Wort Rootstock, Sarsaparilla Rootstock, Potassium Citrate, and Calcium Glycerophosphate, in a base of Sorbitol.

USES: This unique blend of herbal extracts is useful for the entire body. It contains extracts to help with body functions.

179. CHLOROPHYLL

INGREDIENTS: Water (reverse osmosis purified), water soluble chlorophyll powder, and fruit flavor.

USES: A water soluble form of Chlorophyll is used to help the body gain the benefits of the green liquid. It is useful in increasing the production of hemoglobin or red blood cells in the body. It is also used as a healing agent. It can help accelerate healing by stimulating the formation of granulation tissue in abrasions, ulcers and burns. Chlorophyll reduces body odors. It may help reduce the growth of bacteria.

180.   ORANGE BEVERAGE

INGREDIENTS: Vitamin A, Beta-Carotene, Vitamin C, Vitamin B1, Vitamin B2, Niacinamide, Vitamin D3, Vitamin E, Vitamin B6, Folic Acid, Vitamin B12, Biotin and Pantothenic Acid in a base of Fructose, Soluble Fiber, Citric Acid and Fruit Flavors.

USES: This beverage supplies the body with 100% or more of 12 essential vitamins plus dietery fiber. It is very helpful in maintaining a healthy body. Vitamins are essential to health and the average diet is often lacking. The fiber is helpful in reducint the incidence of cardiovascular disease, colon cancer and diabetes. The fiber also helps promote normal elimination.

181.   C-SUPPLEMENT

INGREDIENTS: Seven naturally occuring forms of Vitamin C including Calcium Ascorbate, L-Ascorbic Acid, Dietary Ascorbigens, Dehydroascorbic Acid, Isoascorbic Acid, Calcium Isoascorbic and Ascorbyl Palmitate, and Dietary Indoles, Grapefruit Pectin, and Bioflavonoids.

USES: Vitamin C supplements are thought to activate cleansing enzymes in the colon, and liver. It is also thought to improve the immune response in the body and enhance the body's defense against allergic reactions. It may accelerate healing time for wounds. It can help improve the building and maintenance of collagen for smooth skin and stronger connective tissue. Vitamin C is also known to increase the absorption of iron in the bloodstream. It may improve metabolism and reduce cholesterol and triglycerides.

182.   ENERGY

INGREDIENTS: Glycogen, Vitamin A, Vitamin D, Vitamin C, Vitamin E, Vitamin B1, Vitamin B2, Vitamin B6, Vitamin B12, Niacinamide, Vitamin D. Calcium Pantothenate, Folic Acid, Biotin, Potassium, Magnesium, Copper, Manganese, Iron, Zinc, Chromium, Ephedra Capsicum, Licorice Root, and L-Carnitine.

USES: This formula contains glycogen which is the body's natural form of stored energy. It helps promote the long drive of energy. Glycogen is stored in the liver and muscles and this product helps control a natural time release of energy to maintain necessary blood sugar levels. The vitamins and minerals are organically chealted which makes them easier to use by the body. Studies have shown this combination to increase energy levels.

183.   IRON PLUS

INGREDIENTS: Organic Amino-Acid Chelated Iron, Yellow Dock Root, Vitamin B12 and Folic Acid, Coated with Chlorophyll.

USES: Iron deficiency is common in the world today. Iron is vital to healthy blood and an essential part of the oxygen carrying hemoglobin of the blood. This formula is not constipating and does not cause gastric upset often associated with iron supplements.

184.   ATHLETE TRAINING FORMULA

INGREDIENTS: Glycogen, Complex Carbohydrates, Chelated Minerals and Vitamins, Lipotropics, Amino Acids, Natural Flavors and Colors.

USES: This formula is a high performance beverage containing glycogen. It is a high caloric, all natural, muscle and weight gain formula. The amino acids help promote rapid muscle growth. It is used for sports activities to aid in endurance and increased performance for the serious athlete involved in rigorous exercise.

185.   ATHLETE PERFORMANCE FORMULA

INGREDIENTS: Glycogen, Complex Carbohydrates, Fructose, Citric Acid, Sodium Citrate, Natural lemon and lime Flavors, Vitamins, Minerals, L-Carnitine and Natural Colors.

USES: This formula is great as a fluid replacement beverage before, during and after sustained workouts. It is an excellent source of mineral, fluid and electrolyte replacement. It helps improve endurance by delaying fatigue. It can help reduce muscle cramping during prolonged exercise.

186.   WEIGHT CONTROL 1

INGREDIENTS: Ephedra Sinica, Ilex Paraguairenis, Arruda Brave, White Willow, Licorice, Dandelion, Kelp and GTF Chromium.

USES: This formula is scientifically blended to stimulate the body's thermogenic (fat burning) ability. It can help reduce hunger and promote weight loss through an increased metabolism.

187.   WEIGHT CONTROL 2

INGREDIENTS: Essential Fatty Acids.

USES: The essential fatty acids are important to the body. They help the central nervous system and must be replenished daily. It can help reduce cravings for fatty foods and eliminate hunger feelings. The body needs the good fat to function. It also helps stimulate the use of the bad fats for energy.

188.   WEIGHT CONTROL 3

INGREDIENTS: Complex Carbohydrates, Glycogen, Vitamins, Minerals, Amino Acids, and other ingredients.

USES: This is a meal replacement beverage containing high carabohydrates, low fat and essential vitamins and minerals in a low calorie form. Complex carbohydrates can enter the blood stream slowly because of the time to break them down into sugars.

189.   WEIGHT CONTROL 4

INGREDIENTS: Ginseng, Echinacea, Psyllium, and other ingredients.

USES: This combination helps enhance the immune system. The immune system is the first defense against disease. This product can help support the body's natural defenses.

Bibliography

This is a selection of other books available from Woodland Health Books for those who want to learn more about herbs and natural healing:

Tenney, Deanne

Introduction to Natural Health, 1992, 161 pages

Tenney, Louise

Nutritional Guide with Food Combining, 1991, 237 pages

Health Handbook, Second Edition 1994, 356 pages

Today's Healthy Eating, 1986, 237 pages

Today's Herbal Health, Third Edition, 1992, 377 pages

Ritchason, Jack

Little Herb Encyclopedia, 1982, 126 pages

Vitamin & Health Encyclopedia, 1986, 130 pages

INDEX